Reality. Bytes
Again

More Manageable Bible Meditations for Young People

Julian Hamilton

First published in 1997 by
KEVIN MAYHEW LTD
Rattlesden
Bury St Edmunds
Suffolk IP30 0SZ

0 1 2 3 4 5 6 7 8 9

ISBN 1 84003 070 4
Catalogue No 1500137

Cover illustration by Graham Johnstone
Cover design by Jaquetta Sergeant
Edited by David Gatward
Typesetting by Louise Hill
Printed and bound in Great Britain

Contents

For Mum and Dad

Acknowledgements

There are a number of people who have pushed or helped along the way and I owe them a lot.

Sadie and Sandra for fighting my handwriting and typing the manuscript. Thank you!

Lynda for encouraging me so much to do the project, and David for allowing me to get it done!

No. 22 for giving so much inspiration and wisdom in the whole area of 'life'.

Cheers to those who took the time to read through earlier material and give thoughts and encouragement. You know who you are, so thanks, you made the difference.

Introduction

Somebody, somewhere, sometime, said something like 'Adolescence is a bombshell'. Too right. But although 'they' (whoever 'they' are and whatever 'they' know) say that it is one of the most turbulent times in life, it can also be a huge adventure. There are ups and downs, twists and turns, highs and lows, and you never can tell just what's round the corner. It's not always easy – for you, or for those around you – but it can also be the biggest amusement ride of your life. During my time enjoying being a teenager, I was very good (hmm) and very bad, but it was all me – the experiences were mine.

The great thing about all I experienced and went through is that God was there with me through all of it. Yes, I wandered away, ignored what he was saying, argued, disagreed and broke the rules. But then, that is what being a teenager is all about. I now look back on all the things I did and, although some of them make me cringe and others make me sad, there are so many times I remember which bring a smile to my face. And the thing about it is that even if I wanted to, I couldn't change one bit. So I had to learn that all I have gone through makes me the person I am now. And all I still have to go through will keep my experience of life expanding. All the things I did, right or wrong, have taught me so much about myself and my life. Yes, I still have so much to learn and I will go on making mistakes for the rest of my life, but the fact will always be that through it all I will look to God. No matter how many times I find myself on my knees, cut and bruised, I will always hold on to his hand because having a relationship with God means going through the bad as well as the good, together.

And some of the thoughts and questions I battle with can be found in this book. However, as with the first book, *Reality Bytes*, this isn't a book to be read from cover to cover! Look through the contents and decide which you want to read or even open the book at random and see what happens. But, most importantly, use it to get into the Bible. It's a wonderful book and God speaks to us through it; so if you hear his voice, don't be too surprised.

Stuck In The Middle

HABAKKUK 1:2-3, 5

O Lord, how long must I call for help before you listen, before you save us from violence? Why do you make me see such trouble? How can you endure to look on such wrongdoing? . . . Then the Lord said to his people, 'Keep watching the nations round you, and you will be astonished at what you see. I am going to do something that you will not believe when you hear about it.'

It's so easy to be stuck on being 'you' sometimes. God calls us to do something different and wonderful and we ask ourselves, 'is it really his voice? No, I must be imagining things again. Best keep my head low for a while and keep thinking carefully.' Familiar?

I know people who dive headlong into work. People who dive headlong into socialising. I remember those who worked harder than anyone I knew when I was at school. (They certainly worked harder than me!) I have friends who are committed to a particular sport and they practise and train so much and so hard that it pains me to even think about it. I know others who work for the Church and their commitment is unquestionable; sometimes it's simply amazing (and far too challenging) to watch!

Mr Habakkuk seems fairly cheesed off here. His life is set. The injustice of gloom and misery have set in and he really isn't happy about it. Verse 5 sees it from God's point of view, 'Listen, this is simply amazing. Just you wait, you simply will not believe what I am going to do for this nation.' That's the point; no one would believe it.

Ireland has the chance to have a bright new future free from guns and bombs, weeping families and mindless hatred. Unfortunately so many of us are set on being 'us' that God has a really difficult time getting through, and getting us excited about what could happen. All the violence, injustice, wickedness, strife, lawlessness and suffering that Habakkuk saw, we still see. We, like him, pray for good and for peace. How often do we then look to others to do the changing? If God is really going to bring love and compassion to our homelands, wherever they may be, how is he going to do it without his people? Do you believe what God can do?

Lord,
You have seen this world
　twisted beyond belief.
It's happened before,
　and it will probably happen again.

But, Lord,
Help me do my bit,
　whatever.
I suppose I'd rather watch others mess it up,
　that way I have no responsibility.
But then again,
　that's not what it's about, is it?

Forgive all that is past, Lord.
Let's have this newness of life.

Tears In Heaven

JOHN 11:32-35

Mary arrived where Jesus was, and as soon as she saw him, she fell at his feet. 'Lord,' she said, 'if you had been here, my brother would not have died!'

Jesus saw her weeping, and he saw how the people who were with her were weeping also; his heart was touched, and he was deeply moved. 'Where have you buried him?' he asked them.

'Come and see, Lord,' they answered.

Jesus wept.

Now this really isn't a very manly thing to do, is it? Come on, all this weeping business? I know that it's a good thing for girls to do. They do it a lot. Crying over this film, crying after that song, crying because of this boy, crying because of that boy. Cry, cry, cry, cry, cry! Now OK, I know that's not really true. But it is true that girls are on the whole a lot more sensitive than guys. And because of that, they have gained a reputation for being slightly more prone to tears. So what's going on with Jesus here?

The sisters (Mary and Martha) had tragically lost their brother, and they were understandably upset at this. Jesus appears, and they start to blame him, again that's quite understandable. People have been blaming Jesus for all kinds of hurts for years. But in the midst of all the weeping and grieving and sadness, surely the manly thing to do is to stay calm, not show misplaced emotion, and be strong? And yet, Jesus wept.

But that's Jesus. He was where he needed to be, letting somebody cry with him, and he shared their pain, and their tears. What a wonderful example to 'men'! Especially those whose biggest weakness is a refusal to *show* weakness. Anyway, who says that crying with somebody and helping share their pain *is* a weakness? Surely, it is a strength?

Lord,
　your humanness is amazing.
You got it all so right.
You met people where they were,
　you knew people's needs.
You even cried with them.

Thank you for doing that, Lord.
Thank you for the knowledge
　that I don't hurt alone,
　because you cry with me.

And, Lord,
　maybe it would be good
　if I could show a more human side.
You know,
　not pretending to be unaffected
　by life's hard moments.
Not thinking
　that the proper thing to do
　is to always seem in control,
　of even the most horrible situations.
But simply to aim
　at sharing other people's grief.

That's quite hard for me to pray, Lord,
　because it seems like I have enough of my own.
But if I can help someone, Lord,
Don't let me chicken out.
Thanks.

Down And Out

MATTHEW 26:21-22

During the meal Jesus said, 'I tell you, one of you will betray me'. The disciples were very upset and began to ask him, one after the other, 'Surely, Lord, you don't mean me?'

I'm sure you can picture the faces on the disciples as Jesus drops this bombshell. They were in the middle of dinner, Jesus was probably acting a little strange (remember sending two disciples ahead, and all the donkey business), because he did have a lot on his mind. So in the middle of this Jesus tells them all that some-body in the room was going to betray him. If you had been there, what would your face have looked like? I'm sure some of them nearly choked on their food!

Then comes the drama, all the answers of 'Oh no, not me'. Probably every one of them said something like, 'I won't betray you, I don't care what you think, I won't go'. You'd think they'd have learned something over the last three or so years! We know, with the beauty of a complete account, that when the final disaster happened at the arrest of Jesus they all ran away. They all left.

I heard some interesting and sad statistics the other day. Something like seven out of ten students who have belonged to or been active in their Christian Union at university do not profess a faith ten years on. They have run away. Previously they had enjoyed fellowship, learned songs of worship, prayed, led out-reach even, perhaps they had told Jesus they would never run away. I don't feel qualified to comment on why people may turn their backs. Maybe it's a case of life taking over, the darkness comes in and lights go out. Who knows? But we all face times of doubt.

Remember that the same disciples who were the closest to Jesus and maybe even let him down the most, were the very same disciples who came back and received power. They then carried the news of Jesus to every part of their world.

We can treat the 'fallen' (as we so badly call them in our churches) in a very unfair way sometimes. God doesn't treat them badly, he welcomes them back with open arms. And it is him they have hurt the most.

Thank you for love, Jesus.
Love that goes deeper
   than I can ever understand.
The kind of love
   that allows broken,
   desperate,
   maybe even hated people
   to come into your house.

Forgive me
   for not being as welcoming as you are.

Judging.
Gossiping.
Listening to rumour.

I suppose it's not really fair,
   because we are all your people,
   and because I need to love people
   just like you do.

Help me to do that, Lord.
I might really need that love
   returned some day.

It's Good To Talk

ISAIAH 21:1-4

This is a message about Babylonia. Like a whirlwind sweeping across the desert, disaster will come from a terrifying land. I have seen a vision of cruel events, a vision of betrayal and destruction. Army of Elam, attack! Army of Media, lay siege to the cities! God will put an end to the suffering which Babylon has caused. What I saw and heard in the vision has filled me with terror and pain, pain like that of a woman in labour. My head is spinning, and I am trembling with fear. I had been longing for evening to come, but it has brought me nothing but terror.

Isaiah seems to be having a bit of trouble here! It can't have been easy to give news like that to the people of Israel, and if you read on it gets worse! Depressing stuff for God's elect.

Question: which one of us has *never* felt a bit 'down'? (that's the polite way of expressing it!) Answer: none! Things don't seem to get better, you never see an end to what you're doing, and there is no real light at the end of the tunnel. The pile of stuff to do or sort out just gets bigger and bigger . . . aargh! Know the feeling? Our Almighty couldn't seem less relevant at those times. We seem to forget very easily that God does know, because by some miracle he sees what we see, feels what we feel, longs for things to change as we do, and cries with and for us if we are not man or woman enough to do it ourselves. What do we do? We moan at friends, blame parents, hate school or work and generally make things into a cloud of doubt and gloom. We hardly ever tell God about it, because of course God is too high and mighty and other-worldly to understand our trivial longings – utter rubbish!

God longs for us to tell him, not flag it off onto someone else while tension and bad feelings rise. Why do we think we can only thank God and ask him for things? God is a lot bigger than that, he has a lot more experience and he deserves a lot better from us. God understands. Whenever you feel down, tell him, and whenever you think you've got a bad deal, talk to him about it. Don't try and hide it, because basically, you can't!

Heavenly Lord,
    you told people of long, long ago
    to prepare for pain.

Maybe you've told us
    and we haven't listened.

We feel sometimes that we are twisted,
    our lives are turning inside out.
All we can see is discomfort,
    and despair.

Can I say this to you, Lord?
Will you hear me if I cry?

Thanks.
I knew you would.

Do Your Own Thing. Not!

ACTS 19:1-3

While Apollos was in Corinth, Paul travelled through the interior of the
province and arrived in Ephesus. There he found some disciples and asked
them, 'Did you receive the Holy Spirit when you became believers?'
'We have not even heard that there is a Holy Spirit,' they answered.
'Well, then, what kind of baptism did you receive?' Paul asked.
'The baptism of John,' they answered.

At some stage in your life you must have met some nice, well-
meaning people with lots of big ideas, who just couldn't pull it
off. I remember some who were going to do the biggest things for
God ever, and it was going to be great.

One particular classic was a big rock gig that was to be held for
the ungodly and unruly youth of the neighbourhood. It was even
held away from church premises. The only problem was that the
ungodly youth decided to stay ungodly for a while longer and the
two bands had a great concert, each being the other's audience!

These disciples were in totally the same boat. They had heard
and been excited about Jesus and in their own way had responded.
There would be little doubt that the messenger who brought the
news did so with a huge amount of power and authority. In this
case it was John and we know that because they tell Paul that
they had received John's baptism. Maybe it was as this was going
on that a few of them began to give sidewards glances and adopt
shifty movements, giving away a slight discomfort with the situation, probably thinking, 'we were getting on just fine here, but
this is going to cause some trouble'. Thankfully they didn't run
away but stayed, and it was then that they heard about Jesus and
then the party really began.

We live in a very intolerant society. The many different Churches
tell us a lot of different things, sometimes even going to pains to

explain just how wrong we are. I love and value Methodism –
basically that's an accident of birth – but hey, it's OK! Still, I've
never been short of people who wish to 'enlighten' me as to my
unfortunate state! Thank God for Paul. He doesn't boast about
himself here, he doesn't demolish a system of beliefs in order to
get some good theology in place. He speaks about Christ. It's
great to talk and it's really important to listen, but remember who
our cornerstone is.

Dear God,
    I'd like to thank you for this world,
    for this land where I live,
    and for all the wonderful
    different people
    you've made.

But, Lord,
    if ever I'm moving
    from having you at the centre,
    please drag me back!

I see too many people
    who lose sight of you
    and I don't think I want to be like that.

Whatever I hear,
    whatever I may sometimes say,
    in whatever ways
    I grow and learn in your faith,
    please just stay in the centre of it all, Lord.

Thank you.

Doing The Dirty Work,
And Getting Clean

MATTHEW 25:34-40

Then the King will say to the people on his right, 'Come, you that are blessed by my Father! Come and possess the kingdom which has been prepared for you ever since the creation of the world. I was hungry and you fed me, thirsty and you gave me a drink; I was a stranger and you received me in your homes, naked and you clothed me; I was sick and you took care of me, in prison and you visited me.'

The righteous will then answer him, 'When, Lord, did we ever see you hungry and feed you, or thirsty and give you a drink? When did we ever see you a stranger and welcome you in our homes, or naked and clothe you? When did we ever see you sick or in prison, and visit you?' The King will reply, 'I tell you, whenever you did this for one of the least important of these brothers of mine, you did it for me!'

It never fails to amaze me just how many Christian people there are around the place who seem really happy with the current state of affairs existing in this world of ours. It just doesn't make sense for a Christian to be comfortable! When we read the above passage we realise it is one of the best passages in the Bible for cutting through the trash which some of us have piled on to simple Christianity. We read here what a life of love actually is. Feeding the hungry, giving water to the thirsty, befriending strangers, clothing the naked, looking after the sick and visiting those in prison. What's more, it's not even all that simple (says he as if he finds it easy!) Ask yourself this: if you were in any of the above situations, how would you feel? Take, for example, being naked. Think about it for one minute and try to imagine it. Dirty? Ashamed? Exposed? Nowhere to hide? Just a few possibilities. It's good and fine to give clothes to someone who doesn't have any, but what's more important is to try and help them feel clean and unashamed about who they are. Do you really think that to feel dirty and ashamed you have to be physically nude? I think not, and there's the challenge.

A great philosopher of many moons ago wrote, 'If one has become a Christian, restlessness continues. Christianity is the most intense, the most powerful restlessness. No Christian can remain at rest and secure.' Now what do you think of that?! Christianity *does* give us an assurance for life, but it does not and should not give us a cosy little 'no strife, no hassle' existence. Let's ask ourselves how happy we think God really is with this world? It can be the smallest things that help, especially if we all do them. Tell someone who is having a bad day that you appreciate what they do. Help with the dishes when it's not expected. Buy a sandwich for a homeless person or simply take time to listen. All of these feed, clothe, aid and equip people for life, not just physically but spiritually. Why not try looking for people who are hungry yet have all the food they can eat, or are thirsty with all the water they can drink; a stranger whom you have known for years, or someone as free as a bird, yet trapped in themselves. You probably won't have to look too far.

Dear Father,
   help us to move the balance.
You know we think about things rather a lot.
But then there's doing something about it.

I know, Lord,
   there are people hurting.
They are everywhere.
Even me, Lord, I'm hurting.
I'm not sure exactly how I would describe it,
   but I'm ashamed of it anyway.

Is that like being naked, Lord?
   feeding, giving, sharing.
Not very easy, Lord,
   when it doesn't come naturally!
But I know it makes sense.

Help me to do it,
   and make a difference.

The Simple Truth

MATTHEW 22:34-40

When the Pharisees heard that Jesus had silenced the Sadducees, they came together, and one of them, a teacher of the Law, tried to trap him with a question. 'Teacher,' he asked, 'which is the greatest commandment in the Law?'

Jesus answered, '"Love the Lord your God with all your heart, with all your soul and with all your mind." This is the greatest and the most important commandment. The second most important commandment is like it: "Love your neighbour as you love yourself." The whole Law of Moses and the teachings of the prophets depend on these two commandments.'

The authorities by this time were getting really cheesed off with Jesus, and you can almost hear them swearing under their breath in the above passage. What happened is that they got together again and selected a question that they thought was going to do the trick, and catch Jesus out. You can almost hear them saying to each other, 'I can't wait to see how he's going to handle this one!' (writer's imagination!). The real problem that they were having was that Jesus, the Jew, had not been acting in a very 'Jewish' way, dishonouring the laws that the Pharisees held so dear. Why, he had even picked corn on the Sabbath! So here they come with the question: 'Which is the most important commandment?'

What a great question! It helps me hugely. In this world there are a lot of people who place a very large emphasis on whether or not we obey a certain number of laws. The conditions of the Church. You, of course, have heard them before – don't drink, don't smoke, don't wear certain clothes to church, don't get your ears pierced if you're a boy, don't wear make-up if you're a girl (or boy!), don't go anywhere a good little Christian shouldn't go and, whatever you do, don't say anything naughty! Thank God I get some perspective here; love God, then love your neighbour.

All else falls into place in the light of this. If there is anything that is vital in the Christian faith, this is it. God above all else. Not what others say, not even what we say or do, but God above all else. Of course in the light of this, what could possibly come next except your neighbour?

It's so hard sometimes, Lord.
All the clamouring voices,
     all the differing opinions,
     all the confusion.

All I need is to keep you at my centre.

I know I've tried to push you out so many times,
     and I know I've had other things
     that seem more important;
     like giving up swearing,
     because I thought I couldn't possibly say something bad
     and follow you.

Thanks, God,
     that you don't depend on my good behaviour
     to bring me to you.
I love you, God,
     you are at my centre.

Are You Ready For God? Am I?

PSALM 88:1-2

Lord God, my saviour,
I cry out all day,
and at night I come before you.
Hear my prayer;
listen to my cry for help!

I had what I think was a pretty disturbing experience a while ago; God really used me. It happens now and again you know! And if it can happen to me, then it can happen to anyone, including you!

I've been doing a wee bit of speaking at various things. A while ago about forty of us were having a good old Christian weekend thing and after I had finished the 'speaky' bit, God's Spirit moved in a powerful way and many of us were touched. Unfortunately, I don't think I expected it, and that's always a bad start.

Someone cried, and cried, and cried; they couldn't have been more honest with God. They wanted to be touched, wanted to feel God close, wanted what I and others had been talking about. Boy, did I feel helpless. I saw tears of agony from the soul, a real depth of anguish and I'm so glad God is God and knew how to handle the situation!

Strange, but in a way as these searchers cried out to God, so did I. I really wanted a spirit of peace for them and it came, but not until a lot of cleansing had been done. Honest crying out to God. The writer above knew about it, perhaps we can learn from him. I know I learnt about it that night.

Then came the night it happened to me . . .

Dear Lord,
    it can be pretty confusing sometimes,
    to let you touch me.

I'm not so sure how to listen,
    what to listen for,
    how to respond.

Help me, Lord.
Help me to just be myself,
    openly and honestly,
    the only way I can.

And when I do, Father,
    will you comfort me,
    or is that too selfish to ask for?

Whatever you do, Lord,
    help me let you do it.

Mills And Boon, Eat Your Heart Out!

SONG OF SONGS 8:1-4

I wish that you were my brother,
that my mother had nursed you at her breast.
Then, if I met you in the street,
I could kiss you and no one would mind.
I would take you to my mother's house,
where you could teach me love.
I would give you spiced wine,
my pomegranate wine to drink.
Your left hand is under my head,
and your right hand caresses me.
Promise me, women of Jerusalem,
that you will not interrupt our love.

Woweee! Hot, hot, stuff going on here. Sounds like something taken directly from a Mills and Boon novel, what we term 'the real romantic stuff'. You know the kind of thing – some day under a sea blue sky in some enchanted corner of the universe, your eyes will meet those of your mystical partner across a smoke-filled room. From that moment on you will gaze into the eyes of that person alone, kiss only them and walk along secluded beaches from now into eternity declaring your undying love.

Give me a bucket . . .

So what's the deal with this passage taken directly from the Bible? I get the impression that there is some kind of real love thing going on here. Now I could be wrong, but public affection, going to mother's house, being at peace in each other's arms, all lead to one thing; serious *lurve*! I'm so glad the Bible does talk about it as well because probably you, like me, always thought that the issue was a nasty, dirty thing that good honest, upright Christians just didn't talk about. The other sex, of course, was only out to hurt you in any way they could.

I have to say that when we enter into relationships we do have the opportunity like we have in no other situation to really mess them up. People can get hurt for a very long time, but some day, it can work, it really can happen. We can fall deeply and tenderly in love and be happy when we are there. What's also interesting is that commentators tell us that this book of love is a metaphor for how we, as the Church, can relate to God. Wow! The most stable, comfortable and appreciated closeness we know is being used to describe how we can relate to God. Now *that's* close.

God,
   I love your Bible!
I love the bits that we don't always hear from pulpits,
   like this passage, Lord.
And I love this imagery.

Perhaps, Lord,
   it would be OK simply to ask you
   to be by my side for a while?
Embrace me, Lord.
Hold me in your arms.

Picture This!

LUKE 9:51-56

As the time drew near when Jesus would be taken up to heaven, he made up his mind and set out on his way to Jersualem. He sent messengers ahead of him, who went into a village in Samaria to get everything ready for him. But the people there would not receive him, because it was clear that he was on his way to Jerusalem. When the disciples James and John saw this, they said, 'Lord, do you want us to call fire down from heaven to destroy them?'

Jesus turned and rebuked them. Then Jesus and his disciples went on to another village.

Picture the scene, if you can:

Jesus and the boys out on the road, having set out 'resolutely' to Jerusalem.

Note: Jesus knew what would happen there. How would you have felt?

Then comes a village; a Samaritan village. They hated the Jews and wouldn't let him through their town. Sounds familiar?

Bit of a fight? Angry words? Threats? Stand-off?

But hey, don't panic, the disciples have the answer: 'Fire from heaven on this village!' Yep, that's sure to do it.

And Jesus?

Well, he just says 'No' . . .

. . . and walks to another village.

Good Lord,
deliver us . . .

from ourselves.

Guess What, Joseph?!

MATTHEW 1:18-20, 24

This is how the birth of Jesus Christ took place. His mother Mary was engaged to Joseph, but before they were married, she found out that she was going to have a baby by the Holy Spirit. Joseph was a man who always did what was right, but he did not want to disgrace Mary publicly; so he made plans to break the engagement privately. While he was thinking about this, an angel of the Lord appeared to him in a dream and said, 'Joseph, descendant of David, do not be afraid to take Mary to be your wife. For it is by the Holy Spirit that she has conceived.' . . . So when Joseph woke up, he married Mary, as the angel of the Lord had told him to do.

Well, what would you have done? Imagine your girlfriend (only if you're a bloke of course!) coming and telling you that she was going to have a baby. The answer to the obvious question, 'But how?' isn't as straightforward as you might at first expect:

'It's OK, the Holy Spirit has come upon me.'

'Oh, that's fine then; silly me for asking.'

It's so easy to skip over these stories and forget that there are real people, real emotion and real turmoil involved; flesh and bone. I'm sure Joseph nearly gave birth himself when Mary made her announcement! It actually took an angel to appear to him a little while later to explain the whole thing and help him accept God's will. The really pounding thing on my heart at the minute is that I'm probably a worse listener than Joseph. I can be very stubborn. When all this was happening years ago and the miracle of miracles was about to take place, it still took a couple of angels dressed in the official outfit to convince the people involved. After all, they were only human, and so am I. Perhaps a couple of angels would do the trick . . .

Lord Jesus,
   thanks for the spectacular way
   in which you came.
It's just such an amazing start
   to a fantastic part of world history.

How did Mary and Joseph feel, Lord?
Were they easy to convince?
Did they want to believe straight away?
Or was it as hard with them
   as it is with me?

It's really great to know
   that you did get through to them.
Keep trying with me, Lord.

I'm sorry for not being too good
   at this Christian bit, Lord.

Maybe with just a couple of angels . . .

To The Max!

JOHN 10:7-10

So Jesus said again, 'I am telling you the truth: I am the gate for the sheep. All others who came before me are thieves and robbers, but the sheep did not listen to them. I am the gate. Whoever comes in by me will be saved; he will come in and go out and find pasture. The thief comes only in order to steal, kill, and destroy. I have come in order that you might have life – life in all its fullness.'

Now this is a good picture. Jesus the good shepherd is also the gate, protecting and looking after us, his sheep. (Provided of course we decide to wander in!) The last verse is what I term, 'well cool'! Get this: not only are we affirmed in the fact that God has given us this life, but we are then told that God wants us to live it to the full.

Wouldn't you love to shout this out to all those dull, grey, boring Christians? I bet you can think of dozens and dozens of things that you can't do because you are a 'Christian'. Well here's another: 'Don't be dull!' God *isn't* dull, God's *not* boring. God doesn't watch over us with a huge heavenly baseball bat in one hand and a pocket-size book of 'life's little rules', in the other. This verse in John tells us that God gave us life in order for us to live it totally, with enormous enjoyment and fulfilment, not live it as though we were constantly tiptoeing up the stairs past our parents' bedroom because we were out too late.

There is so much that is pure and good in this world that we should be constantly thanking God for it. I'm sure that if you were pushed you could think of some good in your life! A friend, parent, pet, home? I happen to love the place where I grew up. I don't live there any more, but I still love it. There is a little beach I used to go to (and still do, for that matter), where I have spent many hours talking, listening, swimming, singing, and praying, though not all at the same time of course. It's a good place and a beautiful place, and it comes from God.

Remember the phrase, 'live life to the max'? Well, God said it first. Enter in through the gate, then go and *live* – Jesus says so!

God,
    you're such a cool God!
Thank you.

Not only did you make us,
    and are with us,
    guiding,
    protecting,
    teaching.
But you want us to really enjoy the life
    you have given.

Seems quite hard at times.
I mean there's so much going on
    that I can't laugh at.
But I thank you that you not only stick by me
    in those times and feel my pain,
    but that you actually laugh with me
    and enjoy what life can do.

It's really good to be living like you want us to, Lord.
I remember those feelings of intense relaxation,
    fulfilment, joy, happiness, excitement.
I suppose it all makes sense now;
    that's what life is meant to be like.
Help me live it, Lord.

What a Wonderful World

GENESIS 1:27-31

So God created human beings, making them to be like himself. He created them male and female, blessed them, and said, 'Have many children, so that your descendants will live all over the earth and bring it under their control. I am putting you in charge of the fish, the birds, and all the wild animals. I have provided all kinds of grain and all kinds of fruit for you to eat; but for all the wild animals and for all the birds I have provided grass and leafy plants for food' – and it was done. God looked at everything he had made, and he was very pleased. Evening passed and morning came – that was the sixth day.

This morning I was reliving some teaching practice days by once again being in an RE classroom. 'Wow, what fun, Julian!' Yeah, right! Well, if truth be told (and we all know 'tis good to be truthful) it was quite good fun.

I learned that many teenagers do believe in God and do believe that Jesus walked the earth. Good start you may think. But then, after some good honest discussion, came the almost inevitable questions. 'The Creation? Six days – yeah, right!', 'I'm no monkey', 'If the Bible says it, then it's true!' Just a few of the comments I picked up amidst the increasingly thickening vapour. I really wish I could have taken every single pupil who participated in the discussion to a little lakeside beach I've been to in North America. Because we could have all slept on the sand, and at 5.30am I could have woken everyone up to witness some sights and sounds that have touched me profoundly. The small (and large, for that matter) animals in the forest behind us, the mist rising from the lake, the sun rising above the tree-covered mountain on the opposite shore, its deep orange reflection gently focusing over the whole lake advancing towards our position. Fish jumping, and a beaver on the early shift before breakfast can be spotted by the ripples behind its head stretching forth in a meticulous 'V' eventually reaching the little beach where they merge with the shore. Perhaps then, these students could notice something of the awe and majesty of our beautiful world. Maybe at this point we could all read the verses above and perhaps realise, at last, why God was 'very pleased'.

Lord, you are amazing,
    your world is beautiful,
    and I'm part of it.

We all do so much damage, Father,
    I'm sorry for the damage I've done.
Yet, Lord,
    you keep creating,
    still making things new, every day.

You can even do it with me, Lord,
    all of us here in fact,
    on your earth.

At times the most proud,
    arrogant, ignorant
    and selfish part of your creation.

Lord,
    give me a warmth in your creation.
Help me to look and see you.
Your handiwork,
    your planning,
    your world,
    of which I'm lucky to be a part.

God,
    it is good to be part of your world.
Thank you.

Daddy God

1 JOHN 3:1-3

See how much the Father has loved us! His love is so great that we are called God's children – and so, in fact, we are. This is why the world does not know us: it has not known God. My dear friends, we are now God's children, but it is not yet clear what we shall become. But we know that when Christ appears, we shall be like him, because we shall see him as he really is. Everyone who has this hope in Christ keeps himself pure, just as Christ is pure.

I've some 'little children' in the current family circle and they're so cool. My nieces and nephew are a reminder to me of what life really can be like. I go and hide (where they have no chance of finding me) and I listen as they search the house, shouting my name so hard that it hurts their throats. It also makes the other 'adults' gradually more frustrated as they endeavour to watch the television, listen to the radio, read a book, talk on the phone, or do something else equally as exciting. Of course they don't find me! So what happens is that I creep out from where I am, sneak up behind them or wait until they have come really, really close, and then I jump out with as hideous a monster laugh as possible! You should see it, it's great. First comes the scream which every dog in the neighbourhood picks up, then the laughing as they run towards mummy or daddy with their hands waving aimlessly around their heads. When they get there with me breathing down their neck, they cling ferociously to the leg they have gained for comfort, then finally they turn to look and see where I am. It's at that moment that you can see it, the sparkle and excitement that's contained in life. It's in their eyes, you just can't miss it. The noise, the tension, the running, the energy, it all blends into one huge bundle of life. Then comes the polite request from an adult to 'please go and play in the hall or in the garden'.

We are all called children of God. How hard does the little child left in you have to fight to get out?

Daddy God,
　Hi!
I suppose I'd just like to squat here a while,
　assured that you're here.
Feeling your warmth.

You must get pretty annoyed
　when you've got something to show me,
　and this adult around me
　pretends it's not cool.

The adult in me takes it all in his stride,
　because of course,
　getting older means abandoning childish ways,
　and as we all know,
　'big boys don't do that kind of thing'.

This child wants to come out and play,
　wants to curl up in your lap,
　wants to be really excited
　about all that you have done
　and are doing.
Tell me again, Lord,
　I'm listening . . .

Don't Be Afraid

ACTS 8:1-8

That very day the church in Jerusalem began to suffer cruel persecution. All the believers, except the apostles, were scattered throughout the provinces of Judaea and Samaria. Some devout men buried Stephen, mourning for him with loud cries. But Saul tried to destroy the church; going from house to house, he dragged out the believers, both men and women, and threw them into jail. The believers who were scattered went everywhere, preaching the message. Philip went to the principal city in Samaria and preached the Messiah to the people there. The crowds paid close attention to what Philip said, as they listened to him and saw the miracles that he performed. Evil spirits came out from many people with a loud cry, and many paralysed and lame people were healed. So there was great joy in that city.

I have some very good friends. We get on well and we have a lot of fun together. One day a short while ago, one of them was cutting my hair for me with a pair of shaving clippers. He had to go and see a man about a dog and had to leave before it was finished, so he took off the No. 2 setting, and put down the clippers. Meanwhile one of the girls present offered to finish the job. She picked up the clippers (remember they are now at 'skinhead' setting) and launched into the middle of my head. OOPS! I didn't even have time to be a little bit afraid of what she might do! So there I sat with a wonderfully straight and well-cut bald patch down the centre of my head!

Suddenly being given a disastrous haircut is nothing compared to the fear that some of these early Christians must have felt, especially at the time of the above passage. Persecution had just broken out and the believers were scattered. 'So what happens now?', 'Where do we go?', 'What can I do?'

Verse 4 contains the answer. Rather than feel totally helpless, they lived what they believed. As they ran from Jerusalem they told people what they had seen God do there. The word of God spread. I find Philip in Samaria really interesting. You see, Jews would have a real problem here. Philip, being a Jew, shouldn't have gone anywhere near Samaria, not even within smelling distance! But he wasn't just a Jew. He was a Christian first, and in the power of the Holy Spirit Philip went forward and did wonderful things in Samaria. It all looked so helpless and frightening when the believers had to run from Jerusalem. I'm sure they wondered what on earth they were going to do, but look at the result. By the way, at time of writing my hair has grown back!

Lord,
    we get scared sometimes,
    I get scared.
Maybe there is good reason sometimes,
    although it's not as if I'm facing persecution.
No one wants to seriously damage my health
    just because I believe in you.

I wonder if I would crack
    under the pressure, Lord?
When the chips are down.
I worry about that.

Thank you, Lord,
    for showing a glimpse
    of what can happen
    in my weakness.

Just keep me open to the idea,
    OK, Lord?

All Of Me

PSALM 103:1

Praise the Lord, my soul! All my being, praise his holy name!

Think of that; your whole being praising God. Everything that is you reaching up and out to God. Not one part of you doing anything else but praise God. Wow! This little poem is one that I wrote about letting God take hold of all that I am. So often everything else in my life takes control and there is an imbalance of the reality of my needs and what I think I want. This poem is an attempt to show the struggle that goes on between that inner voice we all know so well, and that need to give everything to God.

The imbalance of reality and want
roams lonely inside my being.
It is a harmful creature,
set upon disharmony and foolishness.
'Take up your sword,' he growls,
'and make your stand.
The enemy will crumble,
they will eat out of your hand.'

For slight moments of ecstasy
I think I can hear it reason.
'I know how you feel,' he pleads.
'Remember we've done this before.'
Oh, I do remember, yes we did.
Waves and fears overpowered my sanity.
And all I could do was cry 'Why'.

This creature will not attack again
from the hollow crevice of my desires.

My being is determined to win at all costs,
and this pain is mental . . . there is no effect.
'But you are the one lying now,' he smirks,
'You are playing my part.'
Yet other ways have I none,
as my being is pulled further apart.

Lord,
  here I am.
This is me;
  nothing less
  and nothing more.

All that I am stands before you.
All that I am reaches out to you.
Every thought,
  every movement,
  every molecule,
  every part of me,
  is yours, Lord.

Use me, Lord.

Wake Up!

LUKE 12:54-57

Jesus said also to the people, 'When you see a cloud coming up in the west, at once you say that it is going to rain – and it does. And when you feel the south wind blowing, you say that it is going to get hot – and it does. Hypocrites! You can look at the earth and the sky and predict the weather; why, then, don't you know the meaning of this present time?'

At times I honestly do like and need the company of good, clean, healthy Christians. I've spent a lot of time with people too like myself! A bit of inspiration has come from actually observing those holy people who, although they sicken me at times because they are so good at the Christian thing, do live earnest and honest lives. Many times I wish I had that kind of spirituality. Alas, I seem to be quite restless and questioning, but that's me, and to be honest, I'd rather have it that way. Jesus, in the above passage, is quite obviously telling the people to shut up and look around. Maybe it's giving my imagination too much licence, but I can picture Jesus in a John Cleese kind of way asking the crowd, 'Are you stupid? Look around!'

I was in a classroom once where a boy had returned to school after being absent for four weeks. He had received a punishment beating, which means that the paramilitary organisation in his area had decided in their 'wisdom' that this boy's behaviour meant he should lose his kneecaps. Not a very nice thing. His teacher asked him if he had decided that he should stop doing whatever it was that caused his beating. His reply, 'Nah Miss, they can't hurt me'. I felt like standing up and shouting, 'Are you stupid, you've got no kneecaps!' But I didn't.

God has given us intellect. He has given us the ability to look around us, see what's going on and decide upon what we see. Take today's news, for example. As I write at this moment, the news consists of police looking for robbers who have stolen £500,000 worth of stock and fled the country; increasing tension in the Middle East; a churchman sent to jail for child abuse; a teenager in court for drugs and a follow-on report saying that almost half of Britain's teenagers take or have taken, drugs. Wake up world!

Lord, I thank you for all that you've given us.
I thank you for the gift
   of being able to look around
   and see what's going on.
It seems so pathetic sometimes.

Why don't more people stand up
   and shout about it?
People killing each other
   all around the world.
It's just pointless.

Lord,
   it's good to know
   that you can see good,
   and that you care, no matter what is going on.

It would be really good
   if more of your people could start to wake up!
I know I don't make a big fuss for you.
Sorry about that, but I know I really want to.
Help me to do that, Lord.

All For One And One For All

1 CORINTHIANS 12:12

Christ is like a single body, which has many parts; it is still one body, even though it is made up of different parts.

I've already written stuff about the camp I worked at in America. Totally cool place; I love it. The name of the camp is Kinawind, and the name means something very special. The first time I heard the story I was sitting on a log by the edge of the water as the sun set over the mountain on the other side of the lake. Since then I have heard it many times and I have even had to tell it. Here it is in condensed form.

The land where the camp is built used to be land that the native American Indians hunted and lived on. In this case, it was the Chippewa Indian tribe. Indian religion shows a great respect for the earth and all its inhabitants and when our camp opened, the leaders wanted to try and hold onto some of that respect for nature. So some of the leaders of the camping community went to speak to members of the Chippewa Indians who were still alive. In talking to the Indians they learnt that in their language there were three words for 'us'. The first, *ninaway*, means 'us over here', but those over there are not part of us, they are excluded. The second word was *ginaway*, meaning 'them over here', but I do not feel part of them, I am excluded. The third word, *kinaway*, from which the camp name Kinawind came, literally means 'all of us together'. That's the body of Christ; all of us together, and I am a part.

Dear Father,
    thank you for this beautiful world,
    and all the things you have put in it.
For all the variety of people here,
    and the people in your Church.

I'm sorry, Lord, for forgetting
    how we are all one under you.

We all matter.
We all have things to do.
We are all different,
    but we are all told to be one.

Help me to remember that, Lord,
    when I get angry at other Christians,
    when I can't see what someone else is saying,
    when all I can think of is me.

Please help me to know
    that I have a part
    in the bigger play.
And that you see the whole;
    all of us together.

I Was Just Sitting There, When . . .

LUKE 18:38-41

He cried out, 'Jesus! Son of David! Take pity on me!'
  The people in front scolded him and told him to be quiet. But he shouted even more loudly, 'Son of David! Take pity on me!'
  So Jesus stopped and ordered the blind man to be brought to him. When he came near, Jesus asked him, 'What do you want me to do for you?'
  'Sir,' he answered, 'I want to see again.'

Try and picture the scene. Jesus is on the road. Probably late in the day, because it was too hot to travel in the middle of the day. The beggar was in his place and there were crowds around Jesus. So, it's late in the day, and lots of people are pushing around to try and get close to this man they had heard so much about.

There's a blind guy begging at the side of the road. He gets excited because lots of people can mean lots of money. He is pushing his hands out and up but in vain, because Jesus is the centre of attraction. But, when he hears the name Jesus, he can't contain himself. He is shouting the name and waving his arms, doing all he can from his scrunched-up inferior position. Someone kicks him and tells him to shut up, Jesus is about to speak.

And Jesus does speak. He asks who it is calling his name. He is looking over the heads of the people telling him that it was them. Then he sees the man still waving and shouting. Jesus asks a couple of the disciples to go and get him. And they do.

Think about it: a man, blind for years. A man for whom begging has become the only way to get a living. He knows no other way of life, blindness is his lot, that's what he is. Blindness defines the man. And Jesus asks, 'What do you want?' You see, even though the man's problem was so obvious, even though everyone, never mind Jesus, could see that what the man needed was his sight, Jesus still asked him. And I think he did it so that the man knew exactly what he did want. It is really easy to get stuck into a way of life that although you want out of it, seems like it is the only way to live. Ever seen *The Shawshank Redemption*? It's a good movie on this theme!

Just make sure you're honest whenever you call upon God and God asks you what you want. Your prayer may be answered.

God,
　you know me better than I do.
And you've seen my future
　before I have,
　as well as knowing the past
　I try to forget.

Help me to know myself better,
　to look at me
　as I really am,
　look for good bits,
　look for things to change.

Then, Lord,
　let me be honest in your presence,
　and ask for the right things.
And more importantly,
　know what to do when you answer.

Give me courage.
Courage to call out your name.
Courage to walk with you all the way.
And courage to really place my trust
　in you alone.

Back To Basics

REVELATION 5:11-14

Again I looked, and I heard angels, thousands and millions of them! They stood round the throne, the four living creatures, and the elders, and sang in a loud voice: 'The Lamb who was killed is worthy to receive power, wealth, wisdom, and strength, honour, glory, and praise!'

And I heard every creature in heaven, on earth, in the world below, and in the sea – all living beings in the universe – and they were singing: 'To him who sits on the throne and to the Lamb, be praise and honour, glory and might, for ever and ever!'

The four living creatures answered, 'Amen!' And the elders fell down and worshipped.

This is not a book of the Bible I read very often. In fact I think I'm just plain scared of it. It's not that I'm not into dreams and visions and stuff, but there really are some weird things going on in the later chapters of the book. But even more difficult than actually reading the book is trying to understand the interpretations various people place on it.

I'm all for interpretation. We need (myself especially) good scholarly people to help us as we look at God's word, but I've met several people who have just turned me off this part of the Bible. I suppose they could be called fanatics – people who try to convince me that every advance in society, every turn our culture makes, is a little twist towards fire from heaven.

Personally speaking, I prefer to think that no one will know the day or hour and that I don't have to understand the ins and outs of Revelation in order to see the hole into which modern society is digging itself. I suppose I just try to deal with what I can see and understand, rather than what I can't see or don't understand.

Having said all that, the passage above is beautiful because I can close my eyes and imagine the glory and majesty of which it speaks. Our God is awesome and deserves wonderful praise, just like that which is pictured. It's powerful, striking, and goes beyond words (because I find it hard to describe!)

Lord, God,
  King of the universe,
  master over all.

May I worship you always,
  with what you deserve.

Praise and glory,
  honour and power,
  wisdom and strength,
  be ever to you, God.

Be ever to you.

Live It!

2 KINGS 16:2

. . . at the age of twenty, and he ruled in Jerusalem for sixteen years. He did not follow the good example of his ancestor King David; instead he did what was not pleasing to the Lord his God . . .

This passage really begs a major question; what is 'doing wrong' in God's eyes? We all know the biggies – murder, adultery, blasphemy, etc. – but is that it?

How about this?

It was Christmas Eve. As usual I had been running around like a madman getting presents for my family, always leaving things until the last minute. It's more fun that way (not!) After it was all done, I went out with some friends to a small social gathering, and then we made our way to our little Christmas tradition: Midnight Communion in the local parish. It's usually really cool – candles, proper choir, real wine (Methodists don't usually get all of these things at the same time!). We had a good service and met a lot of people we would only see once or twice a year. Then it was time to walk outside. Woweee! At last, a foot of snow! Just fallen, all fresh and lovely. My face lit up with excitement. I had never in my life experienced snow so close to Christmas, and here it was! Thick and deep and just crying out to be played in! I was loving it. After a snowball or two I asked around to see who was going to come and play with me? You know what? No one did. People were cold, they had to go home, it was late, they would get wet, blah, blah, blah. I was ashamed. The only time in my life (so far) that I had the opportunity to play in the snow while Santa crawled down my chimney, and no one would join me. The moment passed away all too quickly.

I don't know how far one can stretch a Bible verse before it snaps, and maybe I go too far, but I honestly think that when we refuse to live the life that God gives, then that is also doing wrong in his eyes. OK, so it may mean getting wet sometimes, it may mean going home a little late, it could even mean a night of too many festivities and food, or walking in the cold instead of sitting by the fire. It is out of our comfort zone. It is into the arena of a huge, wonderful life. Live it – God says so!

Wonderful creating God,
    thanks very much for my life.
It's fantastic!

I know I complain a lot,
    keep asking for things,
    always want things to be better.
But I want to say now,
    that life is a good thing to have,
    and you gave it.

Help me to learn more and more
    about how to live it
    to the best of my ability,
That way,
    my life can be pleasing
    in your eyes.
Thanks, Lord.

It's Your Call

John 6:60-66

Many of his followers heard this and said, 'This teaching is too hard. Who can listen to it?' Without being told, Jesus knew that they were grumbling about this, so he said to them, 'Does this make you want to give up? Suppose, then, that you should see the Son of Man go back up to the place where he was before? What gives life is God's Spirit; man's power is of no use at all. The words I have spoken to you bring God's life-giving Spirit. Yet some of you do not believe.' (Jesus knew from the very beginning who were the ones that would not believe and which one would betray him.) And he added, 'This is the very reason I told you that no one can come to me unless the Father makes it possible for him to do so.' Because of this, many of Jesus' followers turned back and would not go with him any more.

I must admit to being a bit lost when I read the above passage. You see, the picture of Jesus which I have in my head is not a Jesus who lets people just wander away. It's a Jesus who bends over backwards for people; he meets their needs, he fills their lives, he knows their thoughts and their dreams and he will do just about whatever he can to make things come together for good for them; but have we another frame to add to the whole picture?

I want to think that as these guys turned their backs, Jesus jumps in and does some spiritual first aid. You know, 'We can talk about this! Let me explain the whole story and help your understanding here.' No. Jesus lets them walk away.

When I attended 'big' school aged eleven, there was a very strong Scripture Union. Within eighteen months, a large number of people in that school year professed to have a Christian faith. Six years later when I left, I could have counted the number from that original group on my fingers. Needless to say, that left many questions for me to chew over in my head. If truth be told, I've still got a load of questions to think over regarding that time of my life.

Now I think I am being a bit unfair to God. I think I used to blame him. Just like when I read about disciples turning away I tend to think, 'Why did he let them do that? What about second chances?' But that only puts the boot on the wrong foot. The decision not to stay involved was theirs and theirs alone. Yes, maybe we all feel we could or should do more for people who struggle in their faith, maybe that's right. At the end of the day, however, I cannot make a decision for anyone and neither will God. The choice is ours.

Loving Lord,
    I find it really hard sometimes
    to look and see people
    just turn their backs on you.

Maybe it's because I think I know
    what they are missing.
Maybe it makes me feel like a failure.

I want to pray now for those people,
    because you know where they are with you,
    and I don't.

Thank you for touching them once, Lord.
I pray that your touch
    is something they can turn back to.

Your warmth.
Your compassion.
Your safety.

Be with them, Father.

Heart And Soul

1 CHRONICLES 16:8-11

Give thanks to the Lord, proclaim his greatness; tell the nations what he has done. Sing praise to the Lord; tell the wonderful things he has done. Be glad that we belong to him; let all who worship him rejoice! Go to the Lord for help, and worship him continually.

I know all of us will have times in life when we look at what has to be done and think, 'Argh! Run away!' It seems that whatever it is – exams, relationships, break-up, career move – it seems to be just that little bit too much to take. I've been asked to go and speak to some leaders in a local church about alternative worship and I find that scary.

The heart of worship, as I see it, is contained in the verses above. Thanking God; telling God in the presence of other people how cool he is; being glad to do it; trying to touch God's heart with what we do. How far removed from that goal is the worship around where you live? Pretty far? Welcome aboard!

It makes me quite angry at times that praise is such a huge area of contentions and ill-feeling in so many churches. Who cares?! If we start to get into an area of argument about what worship is, surely we should be asking, 'What does God think of it?' But we don't. People argue over organs, drama, loud drums, modern techno music. When we do that, and nothing else, we go nowhere. In the words of Coolio, 'Why are we so blind to see that the ones we hurt are you and me?' I think we miss the point. Much of worship is dead because it's rigid, it's meaningless and therefore bears no fruit. To try and change all that, you're talking about a major move of God's power. Maybe that's why I'm scared about talking to church leaders about alternative worship. It's not just a question of changing songs, sound equipment or bringing in a Christian DJ, or whatever. It's a question of touching the heart of God and,

as I see it, that has to be done by me. . . and you . . . and your
neighbour . . . and your neighbour's neighbour . . .

Lord God,
   you are special to me.
I think you are wonderful,
   and I want to make you happy
   with the praise I bring to you.

I know I get frustrated at times in church.
Hymns are too slow,
   prayers are too long,
   words are too big,
   the minister's hair is too short (if he's got any left!)

But I realise that my heart
   is the important bit.
It's not about if I dance or not,
   or if I clap and shout or not.
It's about me trying to make you happy.

Help me to be real with you,
   because there are no disguises
   that you can't see through.
Cheers, Lord,
   you are amazing,
   and I mean that.

Party Politics

MATTHEW 4:23

Jesus went all over Galilee, teaching in the synagogues, preaching the Good News about the Kingdom, and healing people who had all kinds of disease and sickness.

One of the things that draws me to Jesus is his style. No shouting at people to get his message across, no political rallies, no chat shows. Just him as he was; the Son of God going around and showing people the true meaning of love. Leading by example; the Servant King.

Here's a little poem I once wrote when I was thinking; would Jesus have made more impact if . . .

How would you have canvassed for votes, Jesus?
Door to door?
Meet the people while on a soap-box?
Tell the press and hope the party comes into line?

What about mass rallies?
Would you hold some of them?
If you touched as many people as possible,
you could fulfil their dreams then and there.

What about an angel fanfare,
or heavenly fireworks to finish with?
That would really do the trick.
Get the votes.

Just to make sure your message gets across,
you could leave your manifesto with people.
Just in case they forget what you said.
You could even sign some copies.

Oh, and make sure there is a picture of you
holding a small child.
That would really win the votes.

But you never went in for that
did you, Jesus?
It just wasn't your style.

I'm amazed again, Lord,
    about something to do with you.
All that you did . . .
    the way you did it.

Teaching.
Healing.
Listening.
Laughing and crying with everyone
    from small children to old ladies.

And still,
    at the end of your life,
    they shouted for you to be killed.

After all you had done for them.

I suppose part of the reason could be
    that you were not like any politician
    they had ever known;
    you spoke the truth at all times.

Maybe that scared them.

Flame Of Life

PSALM 27:1

The Lord is my light and my salvation;
I will fear no one.
The Lord protects me from all danger;
I will never be afraid.

Confession time! I love fire! There you go, I said it . . . there is no turning back! Although I have never started a big fire deliberately or anything (in case anyone is thinking, 'Ah, he's a pyromaniac!'), I do love fire, but then, who doesn't?

I remember my dad burning all the rubbish in the garden when I was about 5 or 6 years old. We would stand beside it watching the pile of dead grass, leaves and twigs, burn down. Then, whenever the flames got really low, Dad would get me to stand back whilst he sprinkled something (probably paraffin) on the pile, and the flames would reach up towards the sky again. We would always do this at night – the flames brightening up the night sky, spreading light all around.

I've always been fascinated by flames throwing light into dark places. From camp-fires lighting up part of a forest, to beach fires. From a night in the house in front of the fire with no lights on, to 50 young people each lighting a candle and bringing a room or even a field from darkness to light. I love all of it. Candles, fires, flames. Maybe it's got something to do with the power of flames. The Bible talks of fire as a purifying tool. Wow! I also think the 'lighting the way' aspect of fire appeals to me. It brightens up dark places, it guides, it can show the way. And Jesus said, 'I am the light of the world'. That's really comforting. One more thing. I don't know if you have ever sat and looked at a candle for a long period of time, but if you have, you may have noticed that although the candle gives light, often just beside the candle itself there is a shadow, a dark place. Life is full of dark places, but even in these dark places, the Light of the World may not be very far away at all.

Lord God,
   heavenly light.
Fire is such a cool thing!
It cleanses, changes, gives light.
But at times it can be harmful.
It can hurt me.

I'm not sure I understand everything.
Well, I know I don't understand everything,
but some things that hurt can be good.
I learn from my mistakes.

Keep teaching me, Lord.
Thank you for being a light in my life.
Show all the dark places,
   stab at them with flames of light.

Guide me,
   and keep me in your light.
May my soul stay alight.
In you.

Time Out

LUKE 6:17

When Jesus had come down from the hill with the apostles, he stood on a level place with a large number of his disciples. A large crowd of people was there from all over Judaea and from Jerusalem and from the coastal cities of Tyre and Sidon; they had come to hear him and to be healed of their diseases. Those who were troubled by evil spirits also came and were healed.

There is no doubt that Jesus created a fuss. Wherever he went, whatever he did, however he did it, people wanted to see him. They wanted to be touched by him, they wanted to ask him a question. Mothers wanted to know what to do with their unruly children, fathers wanted to see if it was OK in the eyes of God to leave a woman totally alone (they did that anyway). Sick people wanting to be made better, rich people wanting to be justified, religious people wanting any excuse to get rid of him, and maybe a few people wondering, 'Is this the one?' But they kept quiet and watched from the back. People, people, people. Push, push, push. Yet Jesus loved them all. He took time with them, spoke, listened, healed, laughed, cried, fasted and feasted with those who came; and they hardly ever stopped coming. It really must have been hard at times.

So where did his strength come from? It came from Daddy; from 'Abba'. We read about it again and again. Jesus was so busy, and yet he took so much time out. He went away to places of quiet, places of solitude, and he talked to Dad.

Try it. Find space, take time. Take time to be still, to listen, to pray, to think, to be yourself in front of God.

Lord God,
　　Daddy.
Thanks for the gift
　　of being able to see
　　how you handled being human.
I forget sometimes
　　that you really did become like me.
I bet it wasn't easy!
Thank you for doing it,
　　and thank you for reminding me
　　that in the midst of busyness,
　　it's good to get away and be quiet.

Help me to do that, Jesus.
To be like you,
　　to know the value of peace and stillness,
　　prayer and thought.
Help me to make you real in my life.
Thank you for this time out.
Help me to make many more.

Surprised?

MARK 4:41

But they were terribly afraid and said to one another, 'Who is this man? Even the wind and the waves obey him!'

This is quite difficult to do, but try and place yourself in the boat with the disciples. Try and picture a bleary eyed, just woken Jesus who gets out of bed, shouts at the weather, then maybe went back to bed! Just imagine the looks on the faces of the disciples; mouths wide open, eyes out of their sockets! Surprised? I think so!

We do Jesus such a disservice in the modern Church. In him we have the most surprising historical person ever to have walked on the earth. Constantly doing things and saying things that made people elbow their neighbour and say things like, 'What was that?', 'Did he really do that?', 'Look, look, what's he going to do now?' And yet in our Christian circles today, we can be rightly accused at times of being dull, irrelevant, boring and sad. It would be enough to make Jesus turn in his grave – if he'd stayed there!

The kingdom Jesus calls us to is topsy-turvy, inside out and upside down. Crazy! The poor get more than the rich, the meek are exalted, the least are the best, the last are the first, children seemingly have advantage over adults, and the dead are raised to life.

Dull? Excuse me!

Boring? What?

Surprising? Very!

I think we need to be a little more Christ-like, don't you?

Jesus,
    help me to see you afresh.
To see the faces of the people around you.
To feel their excitement
    at seeing you come along the road.
To know the power they recognised
    and worshipped.

It's so amazing to read about you,
    and to know that you want me to be a part of that.
I would love to be excited,
    real,
    rebellious for you,
    but I suppose I get plain scared at times.
Is that alright, Lord?

So many people don't understand
    about the life you lived.

Help me to show others how relevant you are
    to our lives now.

Free Falling

ISAIAH 14:14-15

You said you would climb to the tops of the clouds and be like the Almighty. But instead, you have been brought down to the deepest part of the world of the dead.

Passages like the one above generally make me feel uncomfortable. Maybe that is a good thing! This is the classic biblical passage telling us about the fall of Satan from heaven, and you must admit, it does read well. Like so much of the Old Testament we are left in no doubt as to what the author is trying to tell us, and nearly always there is so much written, that we could spend a lifetime studying it and trying to understand it.

I really haven't had a lot of experience regarding the 'darkness'! You know, demons, etc. (at least not that I am conscious of, but having read Frank Perretti I do wonder!) I've studied religion, conversion, and psychology all together, and I do know a little about the power of the mind. It's the most powerful tool in our body. However, if I believe in a supernatural God and the power of his word, then it seems to run alongside a supernatural power for bad in our world. And having observed some of the things we do to our fellow human beings, I feel there is no natural explanation.

Look at the evil in the above verses. The 'King of Babylon' wanted to be like God. Easy to condemn isn't it?

But think for a minute. Which one of us has never wanted to be better than everyone around? Who has never wished they could have it their own way? Who has never taken control of a situation and felt pride at sorting things out for other people. Who has never wished they did know it all?

That's when we try to be God. When we try to take control we are on the same path that started things going wrong here. Ask Eve; it all sounded so reasonable, just knowledge. But the aim was selfish, and I know I'm as guilty of that as she was.

Daddy God,
   it sounds so dark and condemning sometimes.
And talk of the devil and demons
   just plain scares me at other times.
I pray
   that you can make things clearer for me,
   and protect me.
Thank you for that.

I also know
   that it's not good to blame my failings
   on someone or something else.
And I know you see through me
   when I try to do just that!

I do want to be like you, Lord,
   but only in that I want to try and love people
   as you do.

Please show me how to do that.

Sources

Now that you've read **Reality Bytes Again**, don't forget to pick up Julian Hamilton's other book in this series, **Reality Bytes**. Here are 28 more of Julian Hamilton's meditations and prayers, designed to help you get to grips with the Bible. Remember though: don't be too surprised to hear God speaking to you when you least expect it!